HASSLE-FREE BUSINESS SETUP IN INDIA

HASSLE-FREE BUSINESS SETUP IN INDIA

CA Manish Gupta

Worldwide Published by
Pendown Press

PENDOWN PRESS LLP
An ISO 9001 & ISO 14001 Certified Co.,
Regd. Office: 3767A, Kanhaiya Nagar,
Tri Nagar, Delhi-110035
Ph.: 8130886000, 9650072927
E-mail: info@pendownpress.com
Branch Office: 1A/2A, 20, Hari Sadan, Ansari Road,
Daryaganj, New Delhi-110002
Ph.: 011-45794768
Website: PendownPress.com

Edition: 2024
Price: ₹ 499/-
ISBN: 978-93-6338-864-2

Layout and Cover Designed by Pendown Graphics Team
Printed and Bound in India by Thomson Press India Ltd.

TABLE OF CONTENTS

Insight 2

Insight 3

Insight 4

Acknowledgements

I am deeply grateful for the chance to share my experiences and insights with you. This book is the culmination of years of learning, growth, and dedication. I hope the words within these pages inspire, inform, and resonate with you.

I extend my heartfelt thanks to my father, the late Mr. Anil Gupta, and my mother, Mrs. Pushpa. Your strength and wisdom have been instrumental in shaping my journey and contributing to my achievements.

To my wife, Disha Aggarwal, you are not just my partner but the cornerstone of my strength. This accomplishment would not have been possible without your love and patience.

To my wonderful children, Vanya, your laughter and joy fill my days with purpose and motivation. You inspire me to reach for the stars.

I am also thankful to my partner, Himanshu, and my team (MAG Family), mentors, and the vibrant community of thinkers and doers. Your ideas and help have been very important to me. You've helped me grow and learn a lot. I owe much of my success to your invaluable guidance and encouragement.

A special thank you to my friend, Dinesh Verma, CEO of Pendown Press, and his team for their unwavering support and suggestions throughout the creative process.

To everyone mentioned and those who are not named, your contributions have been vital to my journey. Together, we have built something extraordinary, and I look forward to continuing this journey of growth and success with each of you.

Thank you for being a part of this shared experience.

❖ ❖ ❖

Preface

Starting a business in India is an exciting chance to enter one of the fastest-growing economies in the world. With its diverse market and young population, India offers great opportunities for both local and foreign investors. However, understanding the processes—from registering a company to choosing a bank and following industry rules—is essential for success.

This book is designed to make these important steps easier to understand. Whether you are a foreign investor or a local entrepreneur, you will learn about Foreign Direct Investment (FDI), the differences between the Automatic Route and Government Route, and sector-specific limits on FDI.

We also cover practical steps for registering your business, complying with tax and labor laws, and how long it typically takes to get started.

Choosing the right bank is crucial for your business operations. This book provides insights into how banks in India can help you set up accounts easily and support your financial needs.

With clear language and practical tips, this guide will help you efficiently set up and manage your business in India. Let this book be your helpful companion as you work towards your business goals in this dynamic market.

❖ ❖ ❖

Author's Bio

CA Manish Gupta is an experienced strategist specializing in India Entry and Tax Compliance, with over ten years of experience helping NRI and foreign business owners navigate the complexities of the Indian market. He founded and leads Manish Anil Gupta & Co., Chartered Accountants, where he has assisted numerous clients in establishing their presence in India and optimizing their business operations.

Manish's passion for helping entrepreneurs is evident in his expertise in tax planning, compliance, and business strategy. His solutions-oriented approach provides actionable insights, and his commitment to delivering measurable results has earned him the trust of clients across various industries around the world.

He has supported over 300 companies in setting up and growing their businesses in India, with clients from more than 15 countries. His international experience allows him to understand diverse business cultures and offer tailored strategies that help businesses thrive in India's dynamic market.

Story Behind the Book

Manish's journey began 24 years ago when his family faced financial difficulties and had to leave their small village in Rajasthan for Delhi. The move aimed at better business opportunities, but the family struggled due to a lack of guidance and the cultural differences between rural and urban life. This experience made him acutely aware of the challenges faced by businesses, particularly those coming from abroad, in navigating the complexities of setting up in India.

Throughout his career, he spoke with over 100 foreign companies looking to enter the Indian market. Many were unaware of the policies, incentives, and regulations that could impact their growth. This realization reminded him of his family's early struggles and motivated him to provide the right guidance to businesses entering India.

Having qualified as a Chartered Accountant at the age of 22, Manish dedicated himself to helping businesses overcome challenges and grow. He leads a team of over 30 professionals at his firm, specializing in providing expert guidance across various industries. His rigorous CA qualification gives him a deep understanding of financial strategy, making him a trusted advisor for businesses seeking a strong presence in India.

Recognizing that he couldn't personally assist everyone who needed help, Manish was inspired to write this book. It distills years of experience and knowledge into a comprehensive guide aimed at empowering entrepreneurs with the insights and strategies necessary for informed decision-making and success in India.

As Honorable Prime Minister Modi aptly stated, Chartered Accountants are "nation builders." Embracing this responsibility, Manish aims to extend his support to a broader audience through this book, providing essential tools and insights for success in the Indian market. His goal is to assist 1,000 foreign business owners by 2027, especially as India's economy is projected to become the world's third-largest.

From his small village beginnings to the global stage, Manish is driven by a desire to make a meaningful impact and create opportunities for others.

❖ ❖ ❖

Introduction

India is full of opportunities and is quickly becoming a major player in the global economy. With over 11 years of experience, my team and I have helped more than 300 companies set up and grow their businesses in India.

India's business environment is different, with many types of authorities, approval processes, and a complex tax system. It's important to know how these things affect your business. Starting a business in India is not just about registering a company; it's about using various tax benefits, subsidies, and compliance advantages that can really help your success.

Our goal is to help foreign business owners easily enter the Indian market, be part of the 5 trillion-dollar economy by 2027, and contribute to making India the third-largest economy in the world by 2047. With over 65% of India's population under the age of 35, the country has a young and energetic workforce ready to support growth and new ideas.

India's popularity is also clear from the fact that it has attracted Foreign Direct Investment (FDI) from 161 countries, showing that businesses around the world are eager to invest here. This book will give you the important information you need about growing industries in India, FDI numbers, the best states for starting a business, and why these states are favored.

We invite you to join us on this exciting journey. With our expert guidance, you can smoothly enter the Indian market, with no hassles and a big smile, setting yourself up for success and wealth in one of the most exciting economies in the world.

❖ ❖ ❖

What Readers Say About the Book

From demystifying the myths around Indian compliance to providing step-by-step guidance on remote business setup, this book covers all the crucial aspects that an NRI or foreign business owner needs to know.

– Dragon Park, General Director,
Kocca, South Korea

I was initially overwhelmed by the thought of starting a business in India remotely, but this book laid out the process in an organized and practical way. It truly made my business journey hassle-free.

– Muthu Solayappan, Director,
Plan Optimus, USA

Overview
Why Should You Come to India?

India's economy is taking off, and it's becoming a major player on the global stage. In the past, it wasn't always easy to set up a business here. There was a lot of red tape, corruption, confusing rules, and unclear laws. But things have changed a lot. Thanks to digitization, it's now much easier to start and run a business in India. This makes it a really attractive place for companies from all over the world. With its young and skilled workforce, India has now become a great place for innovation and growth.

Tax Reforms and Simplification

Before 2017, India had a complicated tax system where each state had its own set of tax rules. This made it tough for businesses to expand to other states, as they had to deal with different tax laws. Often, companies needed the help of several legal experts just to understand these rules. The introduction of the Goods and Services Tax (GST) changed everything. By bringing together 29 state taxes into one single system, GST has made the tax process simpler and has made it easier for businesses to work smoothly across the entire country.

Another important change is the introduction of faceless income tax assessments. Before this, people had to personally visit tax offices to handle income tax disputes. Now, with the faceless system, everything happens over a virtual call, making it much easier to explain your case without needing to meet anyone in person. This step has greatly reduced chances for corruption and removed human involvement, allowing businesses to operate honestly without worrying about unfair treatment from tax authorities. These changes have helped create a more transparent and business-friendly environment in India.

Political Stability and Continuous Reforms

India's political stability has played a crucial role in the ongoing simplification of tax measures and other business regulations. The government's commitment to continuous reform has addressed many of the challenges previously faced by businesses. Today, India is a much more reliable and supportive place for companies to grow. The government has worked hard to make things easier and more efficient. They've introduced reforms that address past problems and open up new possibilities.

Vast Consumer Market and Skilled Workforce

With a population of over 1.4 billion people, India has a huge and growing consumer market. The rising levels of consumption create many opportunities for businesses to succeed. India also has a large and skilled workforce that fits well with different industries.

The growth of remote work has made doing business in India even easier. Companies can now hire skilled workers from all over the country, benefiting from a diverse talent pool without being limited by location. This has opened up new possibilities for businesses to grow and succeed across India.

Cash Flow Improvements and MSME Support

One of the key challenges businesses face globally is managing cash flow. India has introduced several measures to address this, including a law mandating that payments to Micro, Small, and Medium Enterprises (MSMEs) be made within 45 days. This regulation has significantly improved cash flow for smaller businesses, ensuring they have the necessary funds to sustain operations and foster growth.

Ease of Incorporation and Business Operations

Incorporating a company in India has never been easier. Advances in technology and regulatory reforms have made it possible for entrepreneurs to start and manage their businesses remotely. Whether you're sitting at your desk in Mumbai or your living room in London, you can handle everything from hiring employees to managing day-to-day operations.

Opportunities For Growth

As a developing country, India presents a unique set of challenges and opportunities. Businesses that address the country's needs and provide solutions to its problems are well-positioned for rapid growth. The combination of a vast market, supportive reforms, and a skilled workforce makes India an ideal destination for businesses looking to expand and succeed.

❖ ❖ ❖

INSIGHT 1

Finding The Perfect Business Structure in India

(1) Basic Business Structures in India

When entering the Indian market, selecting the appropriate business structure is crucialas it determines operational flexibility, tax obligations, and the long-term growth potential of the business. Different structures cater to different business needs, operational scopes, and strategic goals. The main business structures available for foreign business owners and NRIs in India include:

- **Branch Office:** A branch office is mainly set up to help and promote the parent company's business in India. Unlike a liaison office, a branch office is allowed to do business activities in the country. However, it can only perform tasks that the parent company is authorized to do, such as research and development, offering technical support, consultancy services, trading, or working as a middleman between two parties. Its role is to carry out these specific functions to support the parent company's goals in India.

- **Liaison Office:** A liaison office serves as a communication link between the parent company and businesses in India, including customers and vendors. Its main tasks include conducting market research, collecting important information, and sharing these insights with the parent company. However, the liaison office is not allowed to participate in any commercial or trading activities. It purely focuses on communication and gathering information to support the parent company's decisions.
- **Limited Liability Partnership (LLP):** An LLP is often favored for its flexibility and limited liability. In an LLP, partners have limited liabilities, which protects their personal assets from business risks. This structure is suitable for businesses seeking a balance between partnership dynamics and protection from financial exposure.
- **Private Limited Company:** A private limited company is a popular choice for foreign investors and NRIs due to its clear legal framework, limited liability, and ease of raising funds. This structure is ideal for businesses looking to scale up and expand in the Indian market,offering both growth potential and legal protection.

(2) Tax Implications of Different Business Structures in India

Each business structure in India comes with unique tax implications,which need to be carefully considered:

- **LLP Taxation:** LLPs are taxed at a rate of 30%, plus an additional 4% education cess. Unlike private limited companies, LLPs are exempt from dividend distribution tax, making profit transfers to partners more tax-efficient. However, LLPs may be viewed as "pass-through entities"for taxation in the home country, depending on that country's tax laws. This could result in additional tax obligations abroad, especially for foreign partners.
- **Private Limited Company Taxation:** Private limited companies are taxed at a base rate of 22%, with an additional 10% surcharge and 4% education cess, resulting in an effective tax rate of 25.16%. Additionally, distributions to shareholders, such as dividends, may also be taxed at rates between 10% and 20%, depending on the Double Taxation Avoidance Agreement (DTAA) in place with the respective country.
- **Branch Office Taxation:** Branch offices of foreign companies face higher taxes than local businesses, with a tax rate of 40% plus extra surcharges and cess. This can be a heavy tax burden since branch offices are seen as permanent parts of foreign companies. The income earned by the branch office is taxed under Indian corporate tax rules. However, businesses might still get some tax relief through DTAA treaties, which can help avoid paying taxes on the same profits in both India and the foreign company's home country.

- **Liaison Office Taxation:** Since a liaison office is not allowed to engage in commercial activities, it is not subject to corporate income tax. However, it must still comply with reporting requirements, and failure to maintain its non-commercial status can lead to taxation as a permanent establishment. The liaison office's costs, including employee salaries and office expenses, may be borne by the parent company, but these expenses are not deductible in India.

(3) The Key Factors to Choose The Perfect Structure For Your Company

Choosing the right structure depends on various important factors:

- **Subsidiary vs. Independent Company:**
  - A **subsidiary company** is one where the parent company holds shares, making it suitable for businesses planning to offer employee stock options (ESOPs), raise funds, or consolidate financials with the parent entity.
  - An **independent company** is owned by individuals, making it ideal for businesses testing the market without involving the parent company.
- **Management and Control:** For company incorporation in India, at least one Indian director is required. In a **private limited company,** you can appoint a director without making them a shareholder, whereas in an **LLP,** the director must also be a partner. This flexibility makes the private limited structure more suitable for diverse management setups.

(4) LLP vs. Private Limited: Which is Right For You?

Criteria	LLP (Limited Liability Partnership)	Private Limited Company
Limited Liability Protection	Offers limited liability protection to all partners.	Offers limited liability protection to shareholders.
Tax Efficiency and Compliance	Tax-efficient with exemption from dividend distribution tax, but may face complications due to pass-through entity treatment in the home country.	Subject to dividend distribution tax, but offers simpler compliance and better fundraising options.
Growth Potential	Less favorable for external funding and ESOPs	More favorable for growth, especially when raising external funding or offering ESOPs.

(5) Impact of Home Country Tax Regulations on Your Indian Legal Structure

When choosing a legal structure in India, it's essential to consider how your home country's tax regulations will impact your business operations and overall tax liability:

- **Tax Credits and Deductions:** Taxes paid in India, like withholding taxes on dividends or income, might qualify for tax credits or deductions in your home country, depending on the Double Taxation Avoidance Agreement (DTAA) between the two countries. Using these credits correctly can help lower your total tax payments by a good amount.

- **Pass-Through Entities:** For Limited Liability Partnerships (LLPs), some countries treat them as pass-through entities for taxes. This means that the profits are taxed at the individual level instead of at the company level. This could lead to double taxation or a higher tax burden unless managed with tax treaties or good planning. It's important to understand how your home country handles LLPs to avoid unexpected tax issues.
- **Foreign Tax Reporting Obligations:** Additionally, many countries require their citizens or residents to report foreign business activities, which could include filing for any Indian entity's earnings. If you don't follow these reporting rules, you could face penalties or extra taxes. It's important to make sure you report taxes correctly in both India and your home country to stay compliant with global tax laws.

(6) Legal Structures of Business For Foreign Companies/ Non-Residents

Particulars	Branch Office	Liaison Office (Represen-tative Office)	Project Office	Partnership Firm	LLP	Private Limited Co.
Suitability	Suitable for conducting Limited Activities like Import & Export, Support Services, Communication & Representation etc.			Suitable for setting up a full-fledged business segment		
Existence	Exists in Representative Capacity of the Foreign Company			Exists as a Separate Legal Entity		
Objective	Created for Short Term Plans			Created for Long Term Plans		
Time Frame	3 Years	3 Years (For certain segments – 2 Years)	Timeline of Project	NA		

Special Considerations		Prohibited from Commercial/ Trading/ Industrial Activities directly or indirectly in India		Only for Non-Residents, not Foreign Companies		
Incorporation	Foreign Company/ Non- Resident can create such entity on its own			Foreign Company/ Non- Resident shall require minimum 1 Indian Person to create such entity		
Ownership	Non-Resident/ Foreign Company itself owns the entity created in India			1 Non-Resident Individual + 1 Resident Individual	Non-Resident Individual/ Foreign Company + 1 Resident Individual	Non-Resident Individual/ Foreign Company + 1 Resident Individual
Management	Authorized Representative of Foreign Company/ Non-Resident			Partners of the Firm (i.e. both Non-Resident & Resident Individual)	2 Designated Partners (1 Resident mandatory)	Directors appointed by the Share-holders (owners) (1 Resident mandatory)
Income Tax	40 % (Currently Applicable) 35 % (proposed in Finance Bill)			30 %		22 %
GST	NA	Applicable only if Sale/ Purchase activities executed in India		Applicable on all		
Repatriation of Funds Out of India	No Additional Cost but subject to Withholding of Taxes	NA No Business Activities & thus No Funds to Repatriate	No Additional Cost on Repatriation of Surplus after Project Completed	No Additional Cost but subject to Withholding of Taxes	No Additional Cost but subject to Withholding of Taxes	Dividend subject to Tax in hands of Shareholders + Surcharge & HEC as applicable along with withholding of tax

Conclusion

Choosing the right business structure is the foundation of long-term business success in India. Each structure—whether it's a branch office, liaison office, LLP, or private limited company—carries unique benefits and challenges, particularly in terms of tax efficiency, management flexibility, and growth potential. Additionally, understanding how your home country's tax regulations interact with Indian laws is crucial to avoid unnecessary tax burdens and compliance issues.

By carefully looking at these factors and matching them with your business goals, you can create a setup that meets your operational needs while also making the most of tax benefits and setting the stage for future growth. As you move ahead, focusing on these early decisions will help avoid problems and keep your business running smoothly in the Indian market.

Case Study: How LCTS Chose The Right Structure For Expansion

Case Study: How LCTS Chose The Right Structure For Expansion

Client: Jesmond Friggieri, Director, LCTS

Industry: Education Consultancy

- **Apprehensions Before Meeting Manish**
  - **Unsure** about the right business structure for India.
  - **Concerned** about tax efficiency and fund transfers across borders.
  - **Needed** a structure that complied with both Indian and international regulations.
- **What Happened Next?**
  - **Manish advised** on a structure that limited liability and optimized taxes.
  - **Simplified** international fund transfers while ensuring compliance with Indian laws.

- **Provided clarity** on regulatory requirements for smooth operations.

➢ **Results Achieved**

- **Limited liability protection** for directors.
- **Tax-efficient operations** and hassle-free fund transfers for global expansion.
- **Full compliance** with Indian regulations, supporting seamless international operations.

❖ ❖ ❖

INSIGHT 2

Incentives, Subsidies, and Tax Exemptions in India

(1) Types of Incentives or Subsidies Available in India?

Before setting up a business in India, it is essential to be aware of the various incentives and subsidies offered by both the central and state governments. These incentives can significantly reduce costs and improve profitability:

- **Production Linked Incentive (PLI) Scheme:** This scheme is designed to encourage companies to manufacture more in India and rely less on imports. It offers financial rewards to businesses that grow their manufacturing operations in the country. Additionally, various states might provide extra benefits alongside the central PLI scheme, making it even more appealing for businesses to expand their activities.

- **State-Specific Tax Incentives:** States like Maharashtra, Karnataka, Tamil Nadu, and Gujarat provide special incentives, including tax rebates, subsidies, and infrastructure support, to attract businesses. Each state's policies vary, so it's important to research and compare these incentives before deciding where to establish operations.
- **Special Economic Zones (SEZs):** SEZs offer numerous incentives such as tax exemptions, reduced customs duties, and simplified compliance procedures to boost exports and provide world-class infrastructure. These zones provide world-class infrastructure and operational advantages, making them ideal for companies looking to target international markets.
- **GIFT City, Gujarat:** GIFT (Gujarat International Finance Tec-City) is a special zone designed for financial services and IT companies, providing multiple benefits, including tax incentives, state-of-the-art infrastructure, and regulatory advantages. It offers a strategic location for international business operations.

(2) Why Your Registered Office Location Matters For Financial Benefits

Choosing the right location for registering your company in India is crucial, as it can directly impact your eligibility for various state-specific incentives and subsidies:

- **State-Wise Tax Incentives and Production Schemes:** While corporate tax rates and GST are uniform across India, individual states provide different incentives to attract businesses. For example, setting up in Maharashtra might offer tax rebates, while Karnataka could provide subsidies for infrastructure development. The right location can significantly reduce operational costs.
- **Major Business Hubs and Their Benefits:**
  - **Delhi:** A prominent hub with excellent connectivity and resources, offering robust infrastructure for diverse industries.
  - **Mumbai:** Known as India's financial capital, ideal for finance, trade, and entertainment industries.
  - **Bangalore:** India's tech hub, perfect for startups and IT companies due to its vibrant ecosystem.
  - **Pune:** Known for IT and manufacturing industries, offering a balance of quality life and business opportunities.
  - **Chennai:** An industrial and auto manufacturing hub with a growing IT sector.
- **Employee Considerations and Home Registration:** Consider the location where most of your employees are based to reduce relocation costs and enhance employee satisfaction. Registering your company at a home address or using coworking spaces can also minimize initial costs, especially for startups and small businesses.

(3) The Essential Registrations For Claiming Tax Exemptions

To claim various tax exemptions and incentives, certain registrations may be required:

- **Subsidy Applications:** Before making any investments, it is crucial to check for available subsidies from both central and state levels. Platforms like Stand Up Mitra provide valuable information on current government incentives.
- **SEZ Registration:** If you plan to operate within a Special Economic Zone, you will need to register your business with the relevant SEZ authorities to benefit from tax exemptions and other incentives.
- **GIFT City Registration:** Companies looking to operate in GIFT City must comply with the specific registration requirements set by the zone's regulatory authorities.

(4) SEZs and GIFT City: How They Can Boost Your Business

- **Special Economic Zones (SEZs):** SEZs are special areas in India that give businesses unique advantages, such as tax breaks, lower tariffs, and easier compliance rules. These zones are created to help businesses export more by offering top-notch infrastructure and a supportive regulatory environment.
- **GIFT City, Gujarat:** GIFT City is a specialized economic zone focused on financial services and IT industries, providing multiple benefits:
    - **Tax Incentives:** Offers tax holidays and exemptions on various direct and indirect taxes.

- **World-Class Infrastructure:** Equipped with cutting-edge facilities, attracting businesses looking for high-quality infrastructure.
- **Strategic Location:** Positioned as a global financial hub, GIFT City is an attractive option for companies seeking a base for international operations.

Conclusion

India offers many benefits for businesses. These include money back (incentives and subsidies) and tax breaks. You can find these benefits in different parts of India. Some are from the central government (like the PLI scheme), while others are from state governments. Setting up your business in the right place is important. You should also make sure you register your business correctly. This will help you get the most out of these benefits. By taking advantage of these opportunities, businesses can make more money, spend less, and grow stronger in India.

❖ ❖ ❖

INSIGHT 3

Setting Up Your Indian Business Remotely

With advancements in technology and digitization, setting up and managing a business in India can now be done remotely. Here's a guide on how you can handle these processes without needing to visit India:

(1) How to Start a Company in India From Anywhere

You can set up a company in India without having to be physically present. The registration process is streamlined to accommodate remote management. Key steps include:

- **Document Submission:** You can submit important documents like identity proof, address proof, and company registration forms electronically. Indian authorities accept digital submissions, which makes the process easier and more convenient.

- **Online Application for Director Identification Number (DIN) and Digital Signature Certificate (DSC):** To incorporate a company in India, all directors must obtain a DIN, and a DSC is required for document signing. Both applications can be completed online.
- **Name Approval and Company Registration:** Using the Ministry of Corporate Affairs (MCA) portal, you can apply for the approval of your company's name and submit incorporation forms. The entire registration process, from submitting required documents to receiving your Certificate of Incorporation, can be managed online.
- **GST and PAN Registration:** To operate in India, businesses must register for a Goods and Services Tax (GST) number and obtain a Permanent Account Number (PAN). These registrations can also be completed digitally without in-person visits.
- **Hiring Local Representatives:** For ongoing management, consider appointing a local representative or director to handle compliance, regulatory filings, and administrative duties on the ground. They can assist in ensuring smooth business operations.

(2) Opening a Bank Account Without a Visit

Opening a business bank account in India can be done without visiting a bank branch. Most banks offer:

- **Video Conferencing Facilities:** Most Indian banks now provide video conferencing services to complete the Know Your Customer (KYC) process. You can verify your identity in real-time through a video call, making it convenient for foreign nationals and NRIs to open a business account remotely.

- **Online Documentation:** Banks allow you to upload necessary documents, such as proof of identity, proof of address, and business incorporation certificates, through their secure online portals. This eliminates the need for mailing physical copies, speeding up the process.
- **Mobile Banking and Internet Banking:** Once the account is opened, you can manage your business banking through mobile and internet banking platforms. These services include fund transfers, checking account balances, downloading statements, and making international payments, all from the comfort of your location abroad.

(3) Regulatory and Verification by Indian Authorities Remotely

Regulatory and verification processes can be managed remotely:

- **Local Representation:** Appointing a local director or representative in India is one of the most effective ways to manage regulatory and verification processes. This individual can handle tasks such as:
    - **Office Visits:** Conducting any necessary verification visits to your registered office or to meet with regulatory officials.
    - **Document Submission:** Collecting and submitting required documents to relevant authorities on your behalf.

- **Regulatory Compliance:** Ensuring that all local compliance requirements, including periodic filings and inspections, are met.

➢ **Remote Compliance:** Ensure that all documentation and processes are managed efficiently through your local representatives. This includes:

- **Document Handling:** This involves managing the process of sending and receiving documents with different government departments. It includes making sure that all forms and certificates are current and up to date.
- **Regulatory Filings:** Filing annual returns, tax documents, and other mandatory reports with the Ministry of Corporate Affairs (MCA) and other regulatory bodies.

➢ **Digital Submissions:** Many regulatory bodies in India now accept online submissions. This allows for:

- **eFiling:** Submitting forms and reports through portals like the MCA21 portal for company registrations, tax filings, and other regulatory requirements.
- **Online Licenses and Approvals:** Applying for and obtaining various licenses and approvals digitally, reducing the need for physical visits.

➢ **Compliance Tracking Software:** Use software or services that offer:

- **Automated Reminders:** Notifications for due dates and deadlines for compliance requirements, helping you stay on top of obligations without manual tracking.

- **Document Management:** Secure digital storage and management of all regulatory documents and correspondence.

➢ **Government Portals and Helplines:** Utilize government portals and helplines to:

- **Seek Guidance:** Access information and assistance from regulatory authorities on compliance-related queries.
- **Submit Complaints or Requests:** Address any issues or requests related to regulatory processes through official online channels.

(4) Annual General Meetings (AGMs) via Video Call

Annual General Meetings can now be conducted remotely:

➢ **Video Conferencing:** The Indian government allows AGMs to be held via video call, allowing shareholders to participate from anywhere in the world. Popular platforms that support secure and reliable video meetings include:

- **Zoom:** Offers features like breakout rooms, polls, and recording options, enhancing the meeting experience.
- **Microsoft Teams:** Integrates well with other Microsoft products and provides robust security features.
- **Google Meet:** Provides a user-friendly interface and easy integration with Google Workspace.

➢ **Compliance:** This change facilitates easier participation and compliance with shareholder obligations without requiring physical presence.

(5) Managing Operations Locally

Day-to-day business operations can be managed locally without your direct involvement:

➢ **Local Management:** Employ local professionals or partners to handle daily operations and compliance.

➢ **Remote Oversight:** Utilize digital tools and platforms to oversee and manage business activities from abroad.

➢ **Financial Management Systems:** Implement cloud-based accounting software for real-time financial monitoring and management.

➢ **Performance Monitoring:** Employ tools to monitor employee performance and business metrics:

- **KPIs and Dashboards:** Set up Key Performance Indicators (KPIs) and use dashboards to visualize performance data and track progress.
- **Automated Reporting:** Utilize automated reporting tools to receive regular updates on business performance and financial health.

➢ **Operational Efficiency:**

- **Standard Operating Procedures (SOPs):** Develop and document clear SOPs for various business processes to ensure consistency and quality in operations.
- **Automation:** Implement automation tools to streamline repetitive tasks, such as inventory management, customer service, and order processing.
- **Customer Relationship Management (CRM):** Use CRM systems like Salesforce or HubSpot to manage

customer interactions, track sales, and handle customer service remotely.

(6) Filing and Compliances Online

India has digitized many regulatory processes:

➢ **Online Filing:**

- Most regulatory filings, such as tax returns and annual reports, can be completed through online portals provided by the Ministry of Corporate Affairs (MCA) and other regulatory bodies.
- Tax filings and compliance submissions can be handled via platforms like the GST portal and the Income Tax Department's e-filing system.

➢ **Digital Signatures:** Use digital signatures and online forms to simplify and expedite compliance processes.

- Digital signatures are used to sign electronic documents and forms, ensuring their authenticity and speeding up the compliance process.
- They help in reducing errors and fraud while making the submission of documents more efficient.

➢ **Online Compliance Platforms:**

- Many regulatory bodies offer online platforms for submitting compliance reports, including environmental clearances, labor law compliance, and corporate governance disclosures.
- These platforms provide user-friendly interfaces and real-time status updates on submissions.

- **Foreign Trade Compliance:**
  - The Directorate General of Foreign Trade (DGFT) provides an online portal for obtaining licenses and managing foreign trade compliance.
  - This portal facilitates application submissions, license tracking, and adherence to international trade regulations.
- **Regulatory Updates:**
  - Subscribing to newsletters, following official announcements, and using compliance management software help businesses stay updated with regulatory changes.
  - Keeping track of new requirements ensures ongoing compliance and reduces administrative burdens.

Conclusion

In summary, this chapter shows how technology makes it possible to set up and run a business in India from abroad. By using online registration, video calls for opening bank accounts and holding Annual General Meetings, and digital tools for compliance and everyday tasks, entrepreneurs can manage their business activities effectively without being there in person. This easy and flexible approach helps international investors successfully navigate the Indian market without needing to be physically present.

❖ ❖ ❖

INSIGHT 4

Myth About Indian Company Compliances

Many people think that managing company compliance in India is a very complicated task. However, recent reforms and digital advancements have made it much easier. This chapter tackles common misconceptions and explains how these changes have truly improved the situation.

(1) How Digitalization is Revolutionizing Compliance in India

- **Simplification Through Digitalization:**
  - **Introduction of Online Portals:** The Indian government has introduced digital platforms to streamline

compliance processes, reducing the need for physical paperwork and in-person interactions.

- **Unified Online Systems:** Businesses now handle most regulatory requirements through centralized online systems. This shift to digital platforms not only improves efficiency but also enhances transparency, allowing for quicker and more accurate handling of compliance tasks.

(2) The Game-Changer: How GST Simplifies Business Operations

➢ **Transition to GST:**

- **Unification of Tax Regime:** The Goods and Services Tax (GST), introduced in 2017, replaced multiple state-level taxes with a single national tax system. This unification simplifies the tax landscape by consolidating various indirect taxes, such as VAT, service tax, and excise duty, into one comprehensive tax.
- **Centralized Filing:** GST has centralized tax filing, eliminating the need for separate state-level registrations and simplifying the tax compliance process.

➢ **Standardization Across States:**

- **Consistent Tax Code:** With GST, India now has a uniform tax system across the country. This consistency makes it easier for businesses to handle taxes when operating in different states, as they no longer have to deal with different state laws and rules.

- **Types of GST:** The GST framework includes three main components:
    - **Central Goods and Services Tax (CGST):** Collected by the central government on intra-state sales.
    - **State Goods and Services Tax (SGST):** Collected by state governments on intra-state sales.
    - **Integrated Goods and Services Tax (IGST):** Levied on inter-state sales and imports, collected by the central government but shared with the destination state.

(3) Cutting Down Corruption With Faceless Tax Assessments

➢ **Online Processes and Transparency:**

- **Reduction in Face-to-Face Interactions:** The shift to digital processes has minimized direct interactions with government officials, thereby reducing opportunities for corruption.
- **Faceless Tax Assessment:** Many income tax disputes and assessments are now handled online, which helps make the process more transparent and fairer.

(4) Simplified Compliance For Taxes, Withholding, and Other Requirements

➢ **Streamlined Tax and Compliance Management:**

- **Automated Systems:** Compliance tasks related to TDS (Tax Deducted at Source), ESI (Employee State Insurance), and EPF (Employee Provident Fund) are now managed through automated online portals.

These systems reduce manual paperwork and ensure accurate, timely submissions, making the compliance process more efficient.

- **Regular Compliance Requirements:** Monthly and annual compliance filings are now standardized and simplified, including forms and due dates for tax payments and financial reporting.

➢ **Ongoing Reforms:** The Indian government is actively working to make compliance requirements simpler and cut down on unnecessary processes. Recent reforms are focused on streamlining regulatory procedures, so it's easier for businesses to follow tax and financial rules.

Conclusion

In short, this chapter shows that following rules in India is easier than people think. New technology and changes, like online tools, GST, and faceless courts, have made it much simpler. Computers can now do things like TDS, ESI, and EPF, which makes managing rules easier. These changes mean things are clearer and work better. So, following rules in India is not as hard as people say.

❖ ❖ ❖

INSIGHT 5

Understanding FDI Approval in India: Automatic Route vs. Government Route

(1) What You Need to Know About FDI in India

Foreign Direct Investment (FDI) is crucial for India's economic growth as it brings in money, technology, and expertise from international investors. Since India opened up its economy, FDI has been a key factor in driving growth in various sectors. The Indian government has set up two main ways for foreign investment: the Automatic Route and the Government Route. Knowing these routes is important for effectively managing the regulatory requirements.

(2) Which Route is Right For Your Business? Automatic vs. Government

- **Automatic Route:** With this route, foreign investors can put money into Indian businesses without needing to get approval from the Indian government first. Most sectors allow 100% foreign investment under this route, making it a straightforward way to invest. This route is designed to make business easier and attract foreign money with fewer bureaucratic obstacles.
- **Government Route:** For some sectors, foreign investors need to get approval from the Indian government before investing. This is because these sectors are important for national interest or strategy. Investments in these areas are carefully reviewed, and you must get approval from the right government authorities before moving forward. This route is used for sectors with limits or special rules for foreign investment.

To find out which route is right for your business, you need to check the specific FDI rules and regulations for your sector. If your business falls under the Automatic Route, you can invest without needing extra government approvals. If it falls under the Government Route, you'll need to apply for and get the required approvals before making any investments.

(3) Sector-Wise FDI Limits and Restrictions

Here is a summary of various sectors, their FDI limits, and the entry routes:

Sector	FDI Limit	Entry Route
Banking - Public	20 %	Government
Banking - Private	74 %	49 % Automatic, Above 49 %-74 % Government
Insurance	74 %	Automatic
Asset Reconstruction Companies	100 %	Automatic
Credit Information Companies	100 %	Automatic
White Label ATMs	100 %	Automatic
Pension Sector	49 %	Automatic
Agriculture & Animal Husbandry	100 %	Automatic
Plantation Sector	100 %	Automatic
Mining	100 %	Automatic
Petroleum & Natural Gas Refining	100 %	Automatic
Defense Manufacturing	100 %	49 % Automatic, Above 49 % Government
Broadcasting Teleports	100 %	Automatic
Broadcasting Content Services	49 %	Government
Print Media (News)	26 %	Government
Publishing of Scientific and Technical Journals	100 %	Government
Civil Aviation - Airports	100 %	Automatic
Civil Aviation - Air Transport Services	100 %	49 % Automatic, Above 49 % Government
Telecom	100 %	49 % Automatic, Above 49 % Government
Railways	100 %	Automatic

Financial Services Regulated by RBI, SEBI, IRDAI	100 %	Automatic
Pharmaceuticals (Greenfield)	100 %	Automatic
Pharmaceuticals (Brownfield)	74 %	Automatic up to 74 %, Above 74 % Government
Power Exchanges	49 %	Automatic
Construction Development	100 %	Automatic
Industrial Parks	100 %	Automatic
Satellites	100 %	Government
E-commerce Activities	100 %	Automatic
Private Security Agencies	74 %	49 % Automatic, Above 49 % Government
Single Brand Retail Trading	100 %	49 % Automatic, Above 49 % Government
Multi-brand Retail Trading	51 %	Government
Duty-free Shops	100 %	Automatic
Food Products Manufactured or Produced in India	100 %	Government
Cash & Carry Wholesale Trading	100 %	Automatic
Biotechnology	100 %	Automatic
Electrical Machinery and Systems	100 %	Automatic
Food Processing	100 %	Automatic
Ports and Shipping	100 %	Automatic
Textiles and Garments	100 %	Automatic
Tourism and Hospitality	100 %	Automatic

This comprehensive list shows that most sectors are open to 100% FDI, often under the Automatic Route. However, it's crucial to check the specific regulations and requirements for the sector you wish to invest in.

Conclusion

To invest in India, you need to know about the Automatic and Government routes. Most businesses can invest fully under the Automatic route. But for some special businesses, you need the government's approval. By checking the rules for each type of business, you can pick the right way and invest more smoothly.

❖ ❖ ❖

INSIGHT 6

Finding The Perfect Bank Partner For Your Indian Business

(1) How Easily Open Your Bank Account in India

Picking the right bank makes opening a bank account in India much simpler. Choose banks that have easy account setup processes, require minimal paperwork, and handle things quickly. An efficient account setup helps you start your business faster so you can focus on running it instead of dealing with banking issues.

(2) How Global Presence Helps You Do Banking Transactions

A bank with a global presence can significantly ease your banking transactions. It provides seamless coordination between your Indian operations and your home country. This is particularly useful for handling international transactions, accessing customer support in your time zone, and managing your finances more effectively. Look for banks with branches or partnerships in your home country to facilitate smoother operations.

(3) Integration With Accounting Software in India

Banks that connect with your company's accounting software make managing finances easier. This integration helps automate tasks like financial reports, salary payments, and checking transactions. Choose a bank that provides this feature to cut down on manual data entry, reduce mistakes, and make your financial operations more efficient.

(4) Aware About International Transactions

Managing international transactions well is important for many foreign business owners. Choose a bank that offers good rates for currency exchange and low fees for sending money abroad. Make sure the bank provides quick issuance of Foreign Inward Remittance Certificates (FIRC) and Bank Realisation Certificates (BRC) to help with compliance and reporting.

(5) Customer Support Services

Excellent customer support is essential for addressing issues and ensuring smooth banking operations. Choose a bank that provides responsive support during your business hours and offers assistance in your preferred language. Effective customer service helps resolve problems quickly and maintains the efficiency of your banking activities.

(6) Banking Charges

Be aware of the banking charges associated with your account and transactions. Different banks have varying fee structures for account maintenance, international transactions, and other services. Compare the charges and choose a bank that offers transparent pricing and competitive fees to manage your costs effectively.

Conclusion

Choosing the right bank is important for your business in India. A good bank can make it easier to manage your money. They can help you open accounts quickly, do business with other countries, and work with your accounting software. They should also have good customer service. Look for a bank that can help you with international money and has clear fees. This will help your business run smoothly and spend less.

❖ ❖ ❖

INSIGHT 7

The Complete Guide to Company Registration and More

(1) Process of Company Registrations

Starting a company in India involves a well-defined registration process that can be completed online. The key steps include:

➢ **Obtain a Digital Signature Certificate (DSC)**

- **Description:** A Digital Signature Certificate (DSC) is required for filing forms on the Ministry of Corporate Affairs (MCA) portal. All proposed directors or partners must have a Class 3 DSC.

- **How to Obtain:** DSCs can be acquired from government-certified authorities. It ensures the online documents are securely signed.

➢ **Obtain a Director Identification Number (DIN)**

- **Description:** A Director Identification Number (DIN) is essential for individuals who wish to become directors in the company.
- **How to Obtain:** During the company registration process, file the SPICe+ form (Simplified Proforma for Incorporating a Company Electronically Plus). This form allows for the registration of up to three directors. Additional directors can be added later using the DIR-3 form.

➢ **Draft the Memorandum of Association (MOA) and Articles of Association (AOA)**

- **Description:** The MOA and AOA are essential documents for incorporating a company. The MOA outlines the company's objectives, powers, and scope of operations, while the AOA governs the internal management and operational rules.
- **How to Draft:** The MOA and AOA must be prepared and signed by the company's subscribers. These documents need to be filed alongside the SPICe+ form during the registration process.

➢ **Register on the MCA Portal**

- **Description:** The SPICe+ form must be filled out and submitted on the MCA portal.
- **How to Register:** Register as a user on the portal, reserve the company name by submitting two

proposed names in Part-A of the SPICe+ form, and complete Part-B with details about the company's structure and necessary documents.

- **Obtain the Certificate of Incorporation**
  - **Description:** The Registrar of Companies (ROC) will review the application and, upon approval, issue a Certificate of Incorporation.
  - **Details:** This certificate confirms the legal existence of the company. Along with the certificate, the company will receive its Permanent Account Number (PAN) and Tax Deduction and Collection Account Number (TAN) from the Income Tax Department.

(2) Other Registrations Applicable For Your Company

In addition to company registration, certain other registrations may be applicable depending on your business activities:

- **GST Registration**
  - **Description:** Required for businesses involved in the supply of goods or services if their turnover exceeds the threshold limit.
  - **Purpose:** To comply with Goods and Services Tax regulations.
- **IEC (Import Export Code)**
  - **Description:** Mandatory for businesses engaged in importing or exporting goods.
  - **Purpose:** Required for international trade. Not necessary if only providing services.

➢ **Professional Tax Registration**

- **Description:** Applicable for businesses with employees.
- **Purpose:** To comply with state-specific tax regulations on professions.

➢ **Shop and Establishment Registration**

- **Description:** Required for businesses operating a physical location.
- **Purpose:** To comply with local regulations governing business operations.

➢ **ESI (Employee State Insurance) and PF (Provident Fund) Registration**

- **Description:** Mandatory for businesses with a certain number of employees.
- **Purpose:** To provide social security benefits to employees.

(3) How Long it Takes to Get Started

➢ **Time for Company Registration**

- **Description:** The entire company registration process typically takes around 15 to 30 days, depending on the completeness of the documents and the efficiency of the MCA portal.

➢ **Time for Additional Registrations**

- **GST Registration:** Usually completed within 7 to 15 days, provided all required documents are in order.
- **IEC Code:** Typically issued within 5 to 7 days.

- **Professional Tax and Shop Registration:** Timeframes vary by state but generally take a few weeks.
- **ESI and PF Registration:** Registration can take 15 to 30 days.

➢ **Total Time to Start Your Business**

- **Overall:** Considering all registrations and potential delays, the complete process from company registration to operational status might take between 1 to 2 months. Ensure all registrations and compliance requirements are met to avoid any delays in starting business operations.

Conclusion

To start a business in India, you need to do a few things. You need a Digital Signature and a Director ID. You also need to register for GST, IEC, and Professional Tax. Each step takes time. If you plan well and follow all the rules, you can start your business in about 1 to 2 months. This will help you succeed in India.

Case Study: How Kanj Technologies Made its Way From The UK to India

Client: Robin Kanjilal, Director, Kanj Technologies

Industry: IT Support and Manpower Supply

- **Apprehensions Before Meeting Manish**
  - **Two-month delay** due to consultants' lack of knowledge on incorporation.
  - **Lost trust** in consultants after past experiences.
  - **Struggled** to acquire necessary documents for incorporation.
- **What Happened Next?**
  - **Company set up** within 30 days, with regular and transparent updates.
  - **Full document coordination** with landlords handled seamlessly and without hassles.
  - **Quick communication** with full ownership 24/7 over phone/WhatsApp.

- **Results Achieved**
    - **Successful incorporation** completed within the expected time frame.
    - **Seamless setup** with all documentation handled efficiently.
    - **Smooth, hassle-free process** allowed the client to focus on business growth rather than administrative challenges.

❖ ❖ ❖

Client Success Stories

Manish and his team provided exceptional support to us, the South Korean Government, in quickly and efficiently growing our content company in India. Their valuable suggestions for changes in our legal clauses have taken a load off our minds regarding any future issues.

– Dragon Park, General Director,
Kocca, South Korea

With CA Manish Gupta's help, I completed the banking process for my company incorporation in just one day! Now, I can fully focus on growing my business and trust MAG & Co. to handle the rest.

– Mike Chawla, Founder,
IBookkeeper, UK

We couldn't have found a better partner than Manish. His deep knowledge of Russian culture and business practices, along with his understanding of FDI norms in Russia, made everything so easy. He also helped us connect with the right partners, enabling us to grow faster in India.

– Prasun, Director,
CFDGT, Russia

❍ ❍ ❍ ❍

Mr. Manish Gupta's team is reliable and responds quickly every time. They helped incorporate my company in a remarkably short time and even handled negotiations with vendors in India to finalize agreements. Highly recommended!

– Robin Kanjilal, Director,
Kanj Technologies, UK

❍ ❍ ❍ ❍

Before setting up a business, everyone has doubts. But MAG & Co. answered all our questions and educated us before making any decisions. Their expertise and guidance at every step made our business journey much smoother.

– Alice, Legal Head,
Guardian Consultant LLC, Germany

❍ ❍ ❍ ❍

Manish and his team provided excellent guidance and comprehensive knowledge about international business in India. They kept us updated regularly, and we are very happy to work with them. Their support has been invaluable to our success.

– Denis, Director,
CFDGT, Russia

❍ ❍ ❍ ❍

Like many other Korean business owners, I felt uncomfortable and worried about legal and financial matters when entering the Indian market. However, MAG proved us wrong through their sincerity and transparent approach.

– Daniel Park, Managing Director,
UNECO Group, South Korea

❍ ❍ ❍ ❍

Manish and his team didn't just help with incorporation, banking, and setting up an address—they coordinated everything. All I had to do was make a call and discuss with them, and they took care of the rest. It was so easy and hassle-free!

– Jesmond Friggieri, Managing Director,
LCTS, Malta

❍ ❍ ❍ ❍

MAG's team is always approachable. The best part was that they met with us regularly to gain a better understanding of our challenges. Not to mention, they were excellent at solving any issues we faced, making the process smooth and efficient.

– *Pablo, Director,*
Revbio, USA

❍ ❍ ❍ ❍

I initially wanted to work with a local firm, but after meeting Manish, I realized everything can be managed online. He handles everything smoothly, and the quick responses prove I don't have to compromise on quality just because I'm not local.

– *Muthu Solayappan, Director,*
Plan Optimus, USA

❍ ❍ ❍ ❍

Keep the Conversation Going!

Dear Readers,

As we reach the end of this book, I would like to express my deepest gratitude for taking the time to read this book.

Thank you for diving into this book! Your time and curiosity are truly appreciated. I'm confident the strategies shared here will empower you to take bold steps in the Indian market.

Now, you have got two choices:

Option 1: Seize the opportunity and put these insights into action to make a significant impact in the Indian market.

Option 2: Facing any hurdles or need guidance? I'm here for you. Just drop me a message or schedule a one-on-one meeting to get the support you need.

Email Id: info@manishanilgupta.com

Contact No.: 8130561754

Let's collaborate to turn your goals into achievements!

CA Manish Gupta, India Entry and Tax Compliance Strategist

❖ ❖ ❖